EMPEROR PENGUINS
OF THE ANTARCTIC

SARA SWAN MILLER

PowerKiDS
press™

New York

Published in 2009 by The Rosen Publishing Group, Inc.
29 East 21st Street, New York, NY 10010

First Edition

Editor: Amelie von Zumbusch
Book Design: Kate Laczynski
Photo Researcher: Jessica Gerweck

Photo Credits: Cover, back cover, p. 1 (emperor penguins) © www.istockphoto.com/Bernard Breton; back cover (caribou) © www.istockphoto.com/Paul Loewen; back cover (polar bears) © www.istockphoto.com/Michel de Nijs; back cover (seals), pp. 4, 8, 10, 18 Shutterstock.com; back cover (walruses) © Sue Flood/Getty Images; back cover (whales) © Paul Nicklen/Getty Images; p. 6 © Thorsten Milse/Getty Images; p. 12 © Doug Allan/ Getty Images; p. 14 © Ingo Arndt/Getty Images; p. 16 © David Tipling/Getty Images; p. 20 © Colin Monteath/ Hedgehog House/Getty Images.

Library of Congress Cataloging-in-Publication Data

Miller, Sara Swan.
  Emperor penguins of the Antarctic / Sara Swan Miller. — 1st ed.
     p. cm. — (Brrr! polar animals)
  Includes index.
  ISBN 978-1-4358-2742-4 (library binding) — ISBN 978-1-4358-3146-9 (pbk.)
ISBN 978-1-4358-3152-0 (6-pack)
  1. Emperor penguin—Antarctica—Juvenile literature. I. Title.
  QL696.S473M55 2009
  598.47—dc22
                              2008028321

Manufactured in the United States of America

CONTENTS

Emperor penguins are not just black and white. They have yellow and orange feathers around their heads and a bright stripe on their bills.

THE BIGGEST PENGUIN OF ALL

Have you ever seen a penguin? With their black backs and white stomachs, penguins look like little men dressed in tuxedos, or dinner jackets. Although they are birds, penguins cannot fly. Instead, they **waddle** around slowly on land. They are great swimmers, though.

All penguins live south of the **equator**. There are 17 different species, or kinds, of penguins. Emperor penguins are the biggest. They stand nearly 4 feet (1 m) tall and weigh up to 88 pounds (40 kg). Emperor penguins live only in Antarctica, the area around the South Pole. It is very, very cold there.

*The emperor penguins in this colony live on Snow Hill Island,
in the Weddell Sea, off the coast of Antarctica.*

COLD, COLD ANTARCTICA

Antarctica is the coldest place on Earth. In the winter, the **temperature** there can drop to -76° F (-60° C)! The cold wind can blow up to 124 miles per hour (200 km/h). Winter in the Antarctic lasts from June until September. During this time, the Sun does not shine. The penguins live in darkness all winter.

Emperor penguins live in large groups, called colonies. Antarctica is home to around 40 emperor penguin colonies. Penguins in the same colony look for food together and use the same nesting grounds. In all, about 200,000 **breeding** pairs of emperor penguins live in these colonies.

This emperor penguin is preening. When they preen, penguins both spread preen oil and make sure that their feathers are lined up right.

KEEPING WARM

How do emperor penguins stand the Antarctic cold? First of all, they have a thick **layer** of fat under their feathers. This keeps heat in and cold out. Emperor penguins also have four layers of feathers. No other birds have such thick feathers.

The top layer of an emperor penguin's feathers is covered with oil that makes the feathers **waterproof**. The penguins have preen glands at the base of their tails. Preen glands make the oil that makes the birds' feathers waterproof. The penguins preen, or clean their feathers, often. This spreads the oil all over their feathers.

These emperor penguins are tobogganing over the ice. Penguins move much more quickly while tobogganing than while walking.

GETTING AROUND

Emperor penguins have streamlined bodies that are great for swimming. The penguins paddle with their **flippers** and steer with their feet. These birds can dive deeper than 1,800 feet (549 m)! They can stay underwater, holding their breath, for as long as 22 minutes.

As birds go, emperor penguins are fast swimmers. They can swim almost 9 miles per hour (14 km/h). On land, emperor penguins waddle around slowly. They cannot walk faster than about 1.5 miles per hour (2 km/h). Sometimes, when emperor penguins come to a hill, they fall on their stomachs and slide along. This is called tobogganing.

Emperor penguins can catch as many as six fish every
time they dive down into the icy Antarctic waters.

WHAT'S FOR DINNER?

Emperor penguins feed only in the ocean. They would not find anything to eat on land because almost no Antarctic animals live on land. Instead, emperor penguins chase after schools of fish and snap them up in the waters around Antarctica. Emperor penguins also dive deep into the ocean to find tasty squid. Sometimes, they hunt for **crustaceans**, such as shrimp.

In the fall, emperor penguins eat a lot of food to get themselves fattened up for the breeding season. The males especially need to build up a lot of fat because they will not eat for most of the winter.

14

Emperor penguins court before they mate. They bow and swing their heads and make songlike sounds.

BREEDING TIME

In the late fall, emperor penguins make the long trip back to their breeding grounds. The penguins may have to travel 50 miles (80 km) inland, but they always find their old breeding grounds.

Then the males and females begin looking for **mates**. They often try to find the same mate from the year before. The penguins hold out their wings, throw back their heads, and make loud cries. Even though there may be thousands of penguins in a colony, some emperor penguins can find their old mates by the sound of their cries.

Emperor penguin chicks have gray down, or soft feathers. After several months, the chicks' adult feathers grow in. Then they can swim for the first time.

EGGS AND CHICKS

After emperor penguins mate, the female penguin lays a single egg. The male pulls the egg on top of his feet. He covers the egg with a warm piece of skin. Then the female goes back to the sea. All the males huddle together in groups to try to stay warm.

Just as the egg is about to **hatch**, the female returns. She comes back with a stomach full of fish that she regurgitates, or spits up, for the chick. The male goes back to sea to fill his own hungry stomach. After a few weeks, the downy chicks gather in groups, called **crèches**.

When hungry leopard seals or killer whales are nearby, emperor penguins spring out of the water. They know that they will be safer on land.

18

WATCH OUT, PENGUINS!

Emperor penguins have a lot of enemies. The chicks are in danger from giant birds called fulmars. The adult penguins guarding the crèche, called aunties, do their best, but many of the chicks will be killed and eaten.

Out at sea, the penguins are hunted by sharks, killer whales, and, worst of all, leopard seals. When a penguin sees a leopard seal, it panics. It races toward shore, zipping over the **surface** like a porpoise or zigzagging quickly underwater. If the penguin is lucky, it can jump onto the ice in time, but leopard seals are fast and deadly.

Some scientists study emperor penguins. They try to find out how many penguins there are and how to keep these birds safe in our changing world.

PENGUINS AND PEOPLE

Many people are interested in emperor penguins. We wonder about how these birds stay alive in cold Antarctica. Some people make special trips to Antarctica to visit these birds in their breeding colonies. However, this is not really a good idea because visitors can scare them. The penguins are then less likely to care for their eggs well.

There are some emperor penguins in **aquariums** that people can see. In 1980, a chick was hatched and raised by its parents for the first time at Sea World in San Diego, California. Since then, more than 20 emperor penguin chicks have been hatched and raised there.

ARE EMPEROR PENGUINS IN TROUBLE?

People who study emperor penguins think there are now fewer of these penguins than there were several years ago. Part of the problem seems to be that fishermen are catching too many fish. The penguins have trouble finding enough fish for themselves. Another problem is oil spills that are caused by passing oil tankers, or ships. Penguins cannot live when their feathers are covered in oil.

People are also worried because the world is getting warmer. The Antarctic ice where these penguins breed and raise their chicks is melting. Luckily, though, people are studying emperor penguins carefully and trying to find ways to keep them safe.

GLOSSARY

aquariums (uh-KWAYR-ee-umz) Places where animals that live in water are kept for study and show.

breeding (BREED-ing) Making babies.

crèches (KRESH-ez) Groups of penguin chicks.

crustaceans (krus-TAY-shunz) Animals that have no backbone, have a hard shell and other body parts, and live mostly in water.

equator (ih-KWAY-tur) The imaginary line around Earth that separates it into two parts, northern and southern.

flippers (FLIH-perz) Wide, flat body parts that help animals swim.

hatch (HACH) To come out of an egg.

layer (LAY-er) One thickness of something.

mates (MAYTS) Male and female animals that come together to make babies.

surface (SER-fes) The outside of anything.

temperature (TEM-pur-cher) How hot or cold something is.

waddle (WAH-del) To walk slowly while rocking from side to side.

waterproof (WAH-ter-proof) Not able to get wet.

INDEX

WEB SITES

Due to the changing nature of Internet links, PowerKids Press has developed an online list of Web sites related to the subject of this book. This site is updated regularly. Please use this link to access the list:
www.powerkidslinks.com/brrr/penguin/